Praying
for your
Children

**BIRTHING YOUR CHILD'S FUTURE
THROUGH YOUR INTERCESSION**

Atinuke Aderemi

SYNCTERFACE

Syncterface Media
London
www.syncterfacemedia.com

PRAYING FOR YOUR CHILDREN
Birthing Your Child's Future Through Your Intercession

ISBN: 978-1-912896-16-5

Copyright © April 2021

Atinuke Aderemi

Published in the United Kingdom by

Syncterface Media, London
www.syncterfacemedia.com
info@syncterfacemedia.com

This book is printed on acid-free paper

To our dear

Adejeminipe

Our beloved son and brother

You left fingerprints of grace on our lives,
and you will never be forgotten

Contents

A Word from The Author

The Lord has made us custodians of His gifts. Irrespective of whether we are biological, adoptive or spiritual parents, it is our responsibility to commit them into God's hands and pray about their present and future.

The importance of praying for our children cannot be overemphasised, and my prayer is that you will see the fruits of your labour and give all the glory to God in Jesus name, Amen.

Be blessed!
Proverbs 22:6 (AMP)

A Parent's Prayer

Thank You, Father, for making us custodians of Your gift. Sweet Holy Spirit, we ask You to please help us train up our children in the way of the Lord and play our part in helping them fulfil their destiny.

Help us to lay aside our will, plans, and ways and teach our children to take on the will of the Father, His plans and purpose for their lives.

Show us how to teach our children the importance of prayer, seeking Your face, studying Your word and dwelling in Your presence at all times. Open our ears to hear Your every instruction and help us be discerning and sensitive. Lord, always remind us to commit everything to You in prayer.

Teach us to listen to our children and grant us grace and wisdom to guide them along the right path. Help our children see themselves as Your masterpiece; fearfully made, bold, more than conquerors, and greatness achievers.

Thank You Father, for answered prayers.
Amen.

1

Confidence

Psalm 73:26
(New King James Version)

26 My flesh and my heart fail; But God is the strength of my heart and my portion forever.

Prayer

Father, we pray that our children will grow in confidence and fulfil their purpose. We ask that as they draw strength from You, please give them the boldness to do what You ask them to do. Open their eyes to see that there are no limits with You in them; with You, they can reach the highest heights. Lord, we pray that our children will walk confidently with You all the days of their lives, in Jesus' name,
Amen.

Reflections

....
....
....
....
....
....
....
....
....
....
....
....
....
....
....
....
....
....

2

Contentment

Philippians 4:12-13
(The Passion Translation)

12-13 I know what it means to lack, and I know what it means to experience overwhelming abundance. For I'm trained in the secret of overcoming all things, whether in fullness or in hunger. And I find that the strength of Christ's explosive power infuses me to conquer every difficulty.

Prayer

Father, we pray that our children will be content in all things. Open their eyes to see Your goodness in all that You have provided for them. Lord, we pray that our children will not lust after things that will take them away from Your presence, but they will be grateful for what You have given them,
in Jesus' name,
Amen.

Reflections

....
....
....
....
....
....
....
....
....
....
....
....
....
....
....
....

3

Courage

Deuteronomy 31:6
(Common English Bible)

⁶ Be strong! Be fearless! Don't be afraid and don't be scared by your enemies, because the Lord your God is the one who marches with you. He won't let you down, and he won't abandon you.

Prayer

Father, we pray that our children will be bold and courageous to do all You want them to do. Give them the ability to tap into Your strength so that they can overcome any form of weakness. Lord, we pray that our children will not crumble under life's circumstances but will stand firm knowing that You are always with them, in Jesus' name,

Amen.

Reflections

....

....

....

....

....

....

....

....

....

....

....

....

....

....

....

....

4

Dependable

2 Timothy 2:15
(English Standard Version)

15 Do your best to present yourself to God as one approved, a worker who has no need to be ashamed, rightly handling the word of truth.

Prayer

Father, we pray that You will make our children vessels for Your glory; vessels that You can entrust with Your plans. Lord, we pray that they will be reliable and dependable in all they do. We pray that they will diligently study Your word and serve You with all their hearts, in Jesus' name,
Amen.

Reflections

....
....
....
....
....
....
....
....
....
....
....
....
....
....
....
....
....

5

Destiny

Isaiah 46:10
(New Living Translation)

¹⁰ Only I can tell you the future before it even happens. Everything I plan will come to pass, for I do whatever I wish.

Prayer

Father, we pray for our children. We ask that You imprint Your purpose for them on their hearts and open their eyes to see who You have created them to be. We pray that with the Holy Spirit's help, they will know and understand their calling and pursue Your will laying aside every distraction. Lord, we thank You because we know that Your grace is sufficient for our children to reach their destiny and fulfil Your call upon their lives, in Jesus' name,

Amen.

Reflections

....
....
....
....
....
....
....
....
....
....
....
....
....
....
....
....
....
....

6

Direction

Psalm 119:105
(The Passion Translation)

105 Truth's shining light guides me in my choices and decisions; the revelation of your word makes my pathway clear.

Prayer

Father, please shine Your light on our children's way and direct their every footstep aright. Align their lives with Your will and plans for them, and may they learn to wait on You for clarity. Lord, we pray that You lead our children with Your righteous right hand along the path that You have laid out for them, in Jesus' name, Amen.

Reflections

....

....

....

....

....

....

....

....

....

....

....

....

....

....

....

....

7

Excellence

Matthew 5:16
(The Passion Translation)

16 So don't hide your light! Let it shine brightly before others, so that the commendable things you do will shine as light upon them, and then they will give their praise to your Father in heaven.

Prayer

Father, we pray for a Spirit of excellence to rest upon our children. May they do excellently in all that they do. Lord, we pray that with the help of Your Spirit, our children will set excellent standards that will bring glory to Your name, in Jesus' name, Amen.

Reflections

....
....
....
....
....
....
....
....
....
....
....
....
....
....
....
....
....
....

8

Forgiveness

Luke 6:37
(The Passion Translation)

37 Jesus said, "Forsake the habit of criticizing and judging others, and then you will not be criticized and judged in return. Don't look at others and pronounce them guilty, and you will not experience guilty accusations yourself. Forgive over and over and you will be forgiven over and over.

Prayer

Father, we ask that You give our children forgiving hearts; hearts that do not hold grudges, bitterness anger or resentment towards anyone. We pray that they will not hold on to records of wrong done, and past mistakes will not prevent them from moving forward. Father, grant them the grace to forgive themselves whenever the need arises. Lord, above all, we pray that our children will always come to You with repentant hearts and genuinely turn away from acts that are not pleasing to You, in Jesus' name, Amen.

Reflections

....
....
....
....
....
....
....
....
....
....
....
....
....
....
....
....
....

9

Friends

Ecclesiastes 4:9-10
(Common English Bible)

9 Two are better than one because they have a good return for their hard work. 10 If either should fall, one can pick up the other. But how miserable are those who fall and don't have a companion to help them up!

Prayer

Father, please surround our children with the right friends, and we pray that the feet of time wasters be far away from them. We come against every form of negative influence, we bind peer pressure, and we declare that our children will always positively impact the lives of their friends and everyone they come in touch with, in Jesus' name,

Amen.

Reflections

....

....

....

....

....

....

....

....

....

....

....

....

....

....

....

....

....

10

Fruitful

Genesis 1:28
(King James Version)

28 And God blessed them, and God said unto them, Be fruitful, and multiply, and replenish the earth, and subdue it: and have dominion over the fish of the sea, and over the fowl of the air, and over every living thing that moveth upon the earth.

Prayer

Father, we ask that You make our children fruitful vines. Fruitful in their studies, careers, marriages and everything that concerns them. Lord, we pray that our children will flourish and prosper and may they always find favour in the sight of everyone they come into contact with, in Jesus' name,
Amen.

Reflections

....

....

....

....

....

....

....

....

....

....

....

....

....

....

....

....

11

Gifts

Proverbs 18:16
(Complete Jewish Bible)

16 *A person's gift clears his way and gives him access to the great.*

Prayer

Father, we pray for our children to use the gifts and talents You have given them wisely. May their gifts make room for them and bring them before great men. We pray that our children will use their gifts to solve problems and bring about solutions in curious ways. Lord, as the gifts that You have deposited in our children begin to manifest, we pray that Your name will be glorified and many will be drawn to Your kingdom, in Jesus' name,
Amen.

Reflections

....
....
....
....
....
....
....
....
....
....
....
....
....
....
....
....
....

12

Godly Decisions

Psalm 32:7-8
(New International Version)

⁷ You are my hiding place; you will protect me from trouble and surround me with songs of deliverance. ⁸ I will instruct you and teach you in the way you should go; I will counsel you with my loving eye on you.

Prayer

Father, we commit our children's ways into Your hands and pray that You give them listening ears to hear Your voice and seeing eyes to see as You see. We pray that they will make decisions in line with Your will and plan for their lives. May they always wait for instructions from You and not make the mistake of making hasty decisions under pressure. And Lord, talking about decisions, we pray that our children will marry the one who You have set aside for them,
in Jesus' name,
Amen.

Reflections

13

Health

Exodus 23:25
(King James Version)

25 And ye shall serve the Lord your God, and he shall bless thy bread, and thy water; and I will take sickness away from the midst of thee.

Prayer

Father, please keep our children in perfect health physically, mentally and emotionally. Lord, we pray that our children will not suffer from any form of sickness neither shall they be involved in anything that will affect their health negatively such as smoking, alcohol, drugs or any other addiction,
in Jesus' name,
Amen.

Reflections

....

....

....

....

....

....

....

....

....

....

....

....

....

....

....

....

14

Honesty and Integrity

Psalm 119:1
(New Living Translation)

¹ *Joyful are people of integrity, who follow the instructions of the Lord.*

Philippians 4:8-9
(The Passion Translation)

⁸ *So keep your thoughts continually fixed on all that is authentic and real, honorable and admirable, beautiful and respectful, pure and holy, merciful and kind. And fasten your thoughts on every glorious work of God, praising him always.* ⁹ *Follow the example of all that we have imparted to you and the God of peace will be with you in all things.*

Prayer

Father, we pray that our children will always be honest and authentic. Grant them the ability to make Godly decisions and to stand firm on what they believe. May their yes be yes, and their no be no. Lord, we pray that our children will be respectful, and always be known as children of integrity, in Jesus' name,
Amen.

Reflections

....

....

....

....

....

....

....

....

....

....

....

....

....

....

....

....

....

....

....

15

Honour God's Name

Exodus 20:7
(Common English Bible)

⁷ Do not use the Lord your God's name as if it were of no significance; the Lord won't forgive anyone who uses his name that way.

Prayer

Father, we pray that our children will reverence Your name and always hold it holy. We pray that they will honour You in everything they do and that they will understand the power in the name of Jesus,
in Jesus' name,
Amen.

Reflections

....

....

....

....

....

....

....

....

....

....

....

....

....

....

....

....

....

....

16

Humility

James 4:10
(Amplified Bible, Classic Edition)

10 Humble yourselves [feeling very insignificant] in the presence of the Lord, and He will exalt you [He will lift you up and make your lives significant].

Prayer

Father, we pray for our children to cloak themselves with a spirit of humility at all times, and we come against pride and arrogance. Lord, we pray that in everything our children do and everything they achieve, they will always give You all the glory,
in Jesus' name,
Amen.

Reflections

....
....
....
....
....
....
....
....
....
....
....
....
....
....
....
....
....
....

17

Hunger for God

Psalm 42:1
(New International Version)

¹ *As the deer pants for streams of water, so my soul pants for you, my God.*

Prayer

Father, we pray that just like the deer pants for the water, so shall our children long for You. We pray that they will always be in the centre of Your will for their lives; they will be sensitive to Your Spirit, and they will hear Your voice. Lord, we pray that our children find delight in spending time in Your word, worshipping and praising You, in Jesus' name, Amen.

Reflections

....
....
....
....
....
....
....
....
....
....
....
....
....
....
....
....
....

18

Kingdom Treasurer

Deuteronomy 8:18
(New International Version)

18 But remember the Lord your God, for it is he who gives you the ability to produce wealth, and so confirms his covenant, which he swore to your ancestors, as it is today.

Prayer

Father, we ask that You give our children an understanding of Your financial plan for their lives and grant them the ability to make Godly financial decisions. We pray that our children will have a heart for the things of Your kingdom and they will seek Your face and be led by You when it comes to spending money. May they grasp the importance of tithing and giving and, with Your guidance, always sow into fertile ground. Lord, we pray that You grant our children the wisdom not to live above their means and always stay true to themselves, in Jesus' name, Amen.

Reflections

....

....

....

....

....

....

....

....

....

....

....

....

....

....

....

....

....

19

Love

1 John 4:7
(The Passion Translation)

7 Those who are loved by God, let his love continually pour from you to one another, because God is love. Everyone who loves is fathered by God and experiences an intimate knowledge of him.

Prayer

Father, teach our children how to love the way You love. Teach them never to look down on others but to always see their fellow human beings through Your eyes. Anoint their lips to always speak in love, correct and receive correction in love. Lord, we pray that our children will know how much You love them and how precious they are to You, in Jesus' name, Amen.

Reflections

....
....
....
....
....
....
....
....
....
....
....
....
....
....
....
....
....

20

Peace

Isaiah 26:3
(The Passion Translation)

³ You will keep in perfect peace all who trust in you, all whose thoughts are fixed on you!

———————

Prayer

Father, we pray that Your peace will reign in our children's hearts. We pray that thoughts of depression, suicide and anything that is not of You will be far from their minds. We pray that Your peace will flood their hearts and build a barrier against negative challenges and circumstances. Lord, we pray that our children will be known as peacemakers, in Jesus' name, Amen.

Reflections

21

Protection

2 Samuel 22:3-4
(Good News Translation)

³ My God is my protection, and with him I am safe. He protects me like a shield; he defends me and keeps me safe. He is my savior; he protects me and saves me from violence. ⁴ I call to the Lord, and he saves me from my enemies. Praise the Lord!

Prayer

Father, we pray for Your protection over our children. Protect them from making the wrong decisions, protect them from choosing the wrong friends, protect them in their going out and coming in, protect them from being in the wrong place at the wrong time and protect them from any case of mistaken identity,
in Jesus' name,
Amen.

Reflections

....

....

....

....

....

....

....

....

....

....

....

....

....

....

....

....

....

22

Reverence

Psalm 111:10

(English Standard Version)

10 The fear of the Lord is the beginning of wisdom; all those who practice it have a good understanding. His praise endures forever!

Prayer

Father, we pray that our children will reverence Your name. We ask that You guide their hearts and pray that they will always honour Your presence. Lord, let their fear of You be the beginning of wisdom, in Jesus' name, Amen.

Reflections

....

....

....

....

....

....

....

....

....

....

....

....

....

....

....

....

23

Self-Worth

Psalm 139:14
(Common English Bible)

*¹⁴ I give thanks to you that I was marvelously set apart.
Your works are wonderful — I know that very well.*

Prayer

Father, we pray for our children to see themselves
as You see them; fearfully and wonderfully made.
May their priority always be to please You and not
seek the approval of man. Let them find their true
worth in You and not through the eyes of friends and
colleagues. Help them value all the gifts and talents
You have placed inside them. Lord, we pray that they
will not suffer from low self-esteem, mood swings or
depression, but they will be confident in themselves
because their trust is in You, in Jesus' name,
Amen.

Reflections

....

....

....

....

....

....

....

....

....

....

....

....

....

....

....

....

....

24

Strength

Psalms 28:7
(New King James Version)

7 The Lord is my strength and my shield; my heart trusted in Him, and I am helped; therefore my heart greatly rejoices, and with my song I will praise Him.

Prayer

Father, we pray that our children will daily draw strength from You. We pray that You will give them the strength to fulfil Your will for their lives. We ask that in those times when they feel weak and inadequate, they will put their trust in You knowing that in You they stand strong. Lord, may our children understand the strength they have in You and know that they can do all things through You,
in Jesus' name,
Amen.

Reflections

....
....
....
....
....
....
....
....
....
....
....
....
....
....
....
....
....
....
....

25

Success

Proverbs 16:3
(English Standard Version)

³ *Commit your work to the Lord, and your plans will be established.*

Philippians 4:13
(New International Version)

¹³ *I can do all this through him who gives me strength.*

Prayer

Father, we pray for our children. We commit their lives to You and ask You to bless the works of their hands. We pray that they will not struggle or toil, but always rely on Your strength to overcome every hurdle they face. Lord, we pray that You will grant them supernatural success in everything they do, and help them realise that they can do all things through Your Holy Spirit who lives in them, in Jesus' name, Amen.

Reflections

....
....
....
....
....
....
....
....
....
....
....
....
....
....
....
....
....
....

26

Surrender

Matthew 6:33
(Revised Standard Version)

²¹ But seek first his kingdom and his righteousness, and all these things shall be yours as well.

Prayer

Father, we pray that our children will know You; that they will have a personal, intimate relationship with You and You will always be the centre of their lives. We pray that our children will surrender completely to You and seeking Your kingdom will be their number one priority. May Your will be their will and may they desire what You desire. Lord, we pray that our children will submit to Your word daily,
in Jesus' name,
Amen.

Reflections

....

....

....

....

....

....

....

....

....

....

....

....

....

....

....

....

....

....

....

27

Temptation

Matthew 6:13
(The Passion Translation)

13 Rescue us every time we face tribulation and set us free from evil. For you are the King who rules with power and glory forever. Amen.

Prayer

Father, we pray that You will grant our children the power to resist and overcome all forms of temptation. We ask that You teach them to guard their hearts with Your truth. Help them to be disciplined and turn away from things that do not glorify You. Lord, we pray that You will guide our children's footsteps such that they will not walk into temptation,
in Jesus' name,
Amen.

Reflections

....

....

....

....

....

....

....

....

....

....

....

....

....

....

....

....

....

28

Transformed

Jeremiah 24:7
(Contemporary English Version)

7 I will give them a desire to know me and to be my people. They will want me to be their God, and they will turn back to me with all their heart.

Prayer

Father, we pray that You will cleanse our children and turn them away from that which does not glorify You. Lord, we pray that Your light will shine in and through them and that You will be their glory and the lifter of their heads, in Jesus' name,

Amen.

Reflections

....
....
....
....
....
....
....
....
....
....
....
....
....
....
....
....

29

Trust

Psalm 118:8
(New International Version)

8 *It is better to take refuge in the Lord than to trust in humans.*

Prayer

Father, we pray that our children will put their trust in You and not in man. May they learn to lean on the Holy Spirit for guidance and counsel. Lord, we pray for our children to exercise faith at all times, seeking Your face with the confidence that You hear them and are working all things out for their good,
in Jesus' name,
Amen.

Reflections

30

Truth and Sincerity

John 8:31-32
(English Standard Version)

³¹ So Jesus said to the Jews who had believed him, "If you abide in my word, you are truly my disciples, ³² and you will know the truth, and the truth will set you free."

John 17:17
(New Living Translation)

¹⁷ Make them holy by your truth; teach them your word, which is truth.

Prayer

Father, we pray that our children will be sincere in all they say and do, and always tell the truth without fear. May Your word and fear of You guide our children to walk in the light and live right. Lord, we pray that as our children live their lives for You may they never be accused wrongly, in Jesus' name, Amen.

Reflections

31

Wealth

Deuteronomy 8:18
(English Standard Version)

18 You shall remember the Lord your God, for it is he who gives you power to get wealth, that he may confirm his covenant that he swore to your fathers, as it is this day.

Prayer

Father, we pray that You will give our children an understanding of what real wealth is and that it can only be found in You. Grant them the grace to invest and manage their finances wisely, and a heart that desires to give generously into Your kingdom. Lord, above all, we pray that they will not idolise riches, but their focus will remain solely on You, in Jesus' name, Amen.

Reflections

....

....

....

....

....

....

....

....

....

....

....

....

....

....

....

....

32

Wisdom

James 1:5
(The Passion Translation)

5 And if anyone longs to be wise, ask God for wisdom and he will give it! He won't see your lack of wisdom as an opportunity to scold you over your failures but he will overwhelm your failures with his generous grace.

Proverbs 24:14
(New International Version)

14 Know also that wisdom is like honey for you: If you find it, there is a future hope for you, and your hope will not be cut off.

Prayer

Father, we pray for our children. We pray that You will grant them wisdom and understanding in the knowledge of You. Lord, please give them the wisdom to excel in everything they do, and as You have said in Your word, we pray that You will hear them when they cry out to You for wisdom to perform their duties, in Jesus' name,
Amen.

Reflections

....

....

....

....

....

....

....

....

....

....

....

....

....

....

....

....

33

Work and Motivation

Psalm 128:2
(Amplified Bible, Classic Edition)

1 For you shall eat [the fruit] of the labor of your hands; happy (blessed, fortunate, enviable) shall you be, and it shall be well with you.

Prayer

Father, we pray that our children will be hardworking, never shying away from tasks set before them. In everything they do, may they always be motivated to please You. Lord, we pray that Your Spirit will lead our children into the right careers where they will thrive and flourish. They will not struggle or toil, but they will eat the fruit of their labour, in Jesus' name, Amen.

Reflections

....
....
....
....
....
....
....
....
....
....
....
....
....
....
....
....
....

The Salvation Prayer

Dear Father, I know Jesus died for my sins and has risen from the dead. As a sinner, I come before You and ask that You cleanse me and forgive my sins. I accept You as my Lord and Saviour and invite You into every aspect of my life. Teach me Your ways, as I surrender my life to You. Please give me the grace to follow You and obey Your word.

Father, I thank You for my life.
May it always be pleasing to You,
in Jesus' name.

———————

Shoshana Fellowship

Shoshana Fellowship is a ministry birthed to pray for and with couples trusting God for children and women who are hurting.

We come together to pray twice a month and have "Word Works" once a month, where we talk on different topics to encourage and learn from each other. As we pray and have "Word Works", we build our faith and intimacy with God.

Our desire is two-fold; to see couples blessed with beautiful children and to see women healed and whole; confident in themselves and their God-given identity.

Our confidence is that couples will testify of God's faithfulness.

SHOSHANA

shoshanafellowship.com

www.ingramcontent.com/pod-product-compliance
Lightning Source LLC
LaVergne TN
LVHW041235080426
835508LV00011B/1219